To: my I
Y
Thanks for your support

OVERCOMING

A WOMAN WHO CONQUERED STRUGGLES BY TRUSTING AND HAVING

FAITH IN GOD

Enjoy the Read!!

Love Lesmarie

LESMARIE COMBRIE

Overcoming

© Copyright Tarnya Coley 2021

Published by Tarnya Coley Publishing LTD

ISBN 978-1-7397428-1-2

All Scriptures are taken from the NKJV

Tarnya Coley

Table of Contents

LESMARIE COMBRIE

Acknowledgement

I give thanks to God for blessing me with such a wonderful example of a woman to be my mama.

My siblings and Uncle John, who supported me with information I had difficulty recalling.

My children, who listened to me going on and on about this project and helped with technological support.

Uncle Bob, for the legacy that helped to support this project.

My pastor at City Road Baptist Church, who encouraged me to develop my story to share with you all.

Thanks to Tarnya, my publisher.

And to all my supporters.

Prologue

I am giving God honour for allowing me grace, mercy, and strength to write about the life of a great woman of courage and fearless faith. This woman stood on the word of God, especially Psalm 27. She may not be mentioned in the Bible by name; however, she could easily fit the profile of the woman King Solomon refers to in Proverbs 31:10–31. She could even be considered as the woman of Samaria, who Jesus met by the well!

You will not find her name in the history books, even though she could have been. This woman overcame all the struggles life threw at her and emerged as a conqueror, a winner! She placed complete faith and trust in the words, "I had fainted, unless I had believed to see the goodness of God in the land of the living. Wait on the Lord: be of good courage, and He shall strengthen thine heart: *Wait ... on the Lord.*" (Psalm 27: 13–14).

OVERCOMING

This book is about my dearly loved mother. Her life and legacy live on in us, her children, those who knew her and those lives she touched deeply. This book came about because of a project I had embarked on earlier in the year, 2021, which did not turn out as planned. Therefore, I thought, "Why should a good story go to waste?"

Other authors may have written similar stories on courage. However, I believe that my mother's story is unique, and I want to share it with you. In addition, my hope is that this book will be an encouragement to someone who may be experiencing challenges. No matter what you are going through, *don't give up*.

This story is set, for the most part, in Jamaica (JA), West Indies. Those who are familiar with that part of the world will no doubt have a greater understanding of some of the experiences my mother underwent.

Mama is referred to by many names.

She was **Mama** to her children, grand- and great-grandchildren.

Sister Dell to her siblings.

Auntie Dell to her nieces and nephews.

Miss/Sister Lewis to friends and loved ones. Some of her friends called her **Miss Mac**.

She was **Mada/Mama Lou** to most of the young adults from Independence City.

She was even referred to as **Ms Combrie** at some point.

Dell, one of the names Mama was known by, was born to a large family, the fourth of 15 children. Her education was elementary, as it was for most children in those days. She had to leave home at a young age to find work in a more prominent area of the Island — Kingston — as she was born and raised in the country parish of St. Ann. She had to do so to help out financially with her siblings.

As life would have it, a young, vulnerable, naïve woman was and still is, prey to unscrupulous men. Mama had her first of nine children at an early age. The three older ones were cared for and brought up by family members.

She was left to care, single-handedly, for her other children. However, she was never alone, whether she knew it or not. I can only imagine what she felt at times or what she had to go through. Above all things, she believed and *had faith* in her God; that He would see her through. Mama grew up with God-fearing parents and a sound religious background.

In the face of hardship, some people take a fatalistic view of life, believing that their plight is just their lot; not my mother. She was a fighter, and even though her life was tough, she was determined to give her children the very best she could afford.

"I can do all through Christ who gives me strength" (Philippians 4:13) was one of her favourite passages from the scriptures. She kept going like a fearless foe, embracing the words of Psalm 27:3: "Though a host should encamp against me, my heart will not fear: though war should rise against me … I will be confident," and confident she was!

Have you ever felt alone, really alone!?

How many times must she have the felt expression of Psalm 27:10, "When my father and mother forsake me; then the LORD will take me up." My! What a place to be.

Mama loved her children and cared for them thoroughly. Her love was sacrificial to the point of giving up what could be seen as an opportunity for a better life, travelling to the USA. A woman of faith and courage, an overcomer, she put her trust and faith in her God as the Psalmist says, "... don't let me be put to shame, nor my enemies triumph over me" (Psalm 25:2). She also knew that her God was a present help in times of trouble.

The Bible tells us in 2 Corinthians 9:7, God loves a cheerful giver. The Greek word for cheerful "*hilros*" (joyous) also means a sense of readiness, of being ready to act at a moment's notice. Mama was always ready and willing to give. When we give in this way, it comes back to us, "pressed down, shaken together and running over" (Luke 6:38). *WOW!* This was one of Mama's strong character traits: Giving.

As you read this book, I hope that you will see the real heart of my mother. The forgiving heart of a woman who was left to raise her five children. I can only imagine the pain she endured, yet she was never known to speak ill of our father to us. Unlike some women, she never used her children as pawns to get her own way. Mama knew she had a God who was bigger than any man and any circumstances. The Lord promised in Joel 2:25, "I will restore to you the years the cankerworm and the locusts have eaten ... my people never be put to shame," so she knew that God heard her voice when she called to Him. He was merciful to her and answered her prayers.

Throughout her struggles, Mama stood firmly on the words of Psalm 27. She knew that her struggles were not going to be the end of her, so she fought on and did not let them define her.

No doubt she experienced feelings of:

- Despondency
- Heaviness
- Depression
- Despair
- Restlessness
- Agitation
- Discouragement
- Frustration
- Psychological bankruptcy

But she never let us kids see it. She leaned on the Lord for strength. She never allowed her struggle to take away her joy. She knew her God was going to do a new thing in her life. She may have even prayed like Paul, in the book of 2 Corinthians, her struggles away. God's grace was sufficient, so she held on by faith, standing on God's words, not her own understanding of what she was undergoing.

Then God favoured her. Hallelujah! God favoured her. Life took a turn. Her struggles were not over, but they were eased. We moved to a brand new home in a new community. Surely goodness and mercy had followed her.

Mother remained confident that she would see the goodness of God. Her children grew up and became upstanding citizens of society. A sad part of her story is that she died before she found out that one of her sons had reached the pinnacle of his profession as an Attorney General in Tortola, British Virgin Islands. We just wanted to ring Mama to give her the good news!

Mama left an undeniable legacy to her children.

- Discipline — her motto was "never spare the rod and spoil the child."

- Strength of character — her life epitomises that.

- Respect — not just for ourselves, but for others.

- Moral standing

- Honesty

- Above all: the love for God.

She left us believing that God will come through if we only trust Him, believe His Word, and lean not on our own understanding.

When Mama finally began a true relationship with her God, like David, she asked for just one thing — to dwell in the house of God all the days of her life.

If you are reading this and are faced with challenges that you do not know how to resolve, take heart; you too can overcome them. Find comfort in the word of God. He is the One who brought Mama through, and He will do the same for you, too.

Psalm 27

Mama's favourite scripture

¹ The LORD is my light and my salvation —
whom shall I fear?
The LORD is the stronghold of my life —
of whom shall I be afraid?

² When the wicked advance against me
to devour[a] me,
it is my enemies and my foes
who will stumble and fall.
³ Though an army besiege me,
my heart will not fear;
though war break out against me,
even then, I will be confident.

⁴ One thing I ask from the LORD,
this only do I seek:
that I may dwell in the house of the LORD
all the days of my life,
to gaze on the beauty of the LORD
and to seek him in his temple.
⁵ For in the day of trouble
he will keep me safe in his dwelling;

he will hide me in the shelter of his sacred tent
and set me high upon a rock.

⁶ Then my head will be exalted
above the enemies who surround me;
at his sacred tent I will sacrifice with shouts of
joy;
I will sing and make music to the LORD.

⁷ Hear my voice when I call, LORD;
be merciful to me and answer me.
⁸ My heart says of you, "Seek his face!"
Your face, LORD, I will seek.
⁹ Do not hide Your face from me,
do not turn Your servant away in anger;
You have been my helper.
Do not reject me or forsake me,
God, my Saviour.
¹⁰ Though my father and mother forsake me,
the LORD will receive me.
¹¹ Teach me Your way, LORD;
lead me in a straight path
because of my oppressors.
¹² Do not turn me over to the desire of my foes,
for false witnesses rise up against me,
spouting malicious accusations.

¹³ I remain confident of this:
I will see the goodness of the LORD

in the land of the living.
[14] Wait for the LORD;
be strong and take heart
and wait for the LORD.

OVERCOMING

1960

Ruth Agatha Mckoy

Part one

RUTH AGATHA MCKOY

"I watch in hope for my LORD, I wait for God my Saviour: my God will hear me." (Micah 7:7)

Ruth was born in January 1930 to Edna and Ira Mckoy in the district of Lime Tree Gardens parish of St Ann, Jamaica. She was born into a large family, the fourth of 15 children. I have been told by my uncles and aunts that as a child, my mother was a feisty girl but very caring, loving and protective of her siblings, a trait that she carried over to the parenting of her own children.

Mama's childhood was typical of children growing up in the rural districts. Her dad was a farmer and had plenty of land. The property where the house is situated is approximately two and a half acres. This was Grandpa's family property. He also had other properties, which was where he farmed his ground provisions and kept the animals. The ground provisions Grandpa farmed included a variety of yams, such as yellow yam, dasheen, white yam and st vincent. He also grew sweet potatoes, cassava, and coco. There were also lots of fruit trees — oranges, mangoes, avocado, jackfruit, apples, grapefruit, tangerines, and limes. Pimento and coffee was also part of what he grew. These foods were grown free of pesticides and fertilisation. All organic.

In addition to the ground provision, Grandpa had animals. He had goats, pigs, cows, rabbits, and chickens, along with his faithful mule/donkey taking him to the field and back.

Mama and her siblings had to do chores like taking the animals out to the fields, milking the cows and meeting the milk truck in the mornings before going off to school, which commenced at 9 a.m. They would be up by about 4 a.m. to get these chores completed. The distance they had to go was not just a stone's throw away. Also, these were not paved roads, but "tracks." They had to walk to get to where they were going; therefore, they had to wake before the cock started crowing to get their chores done. Since there was no electricity or street lighting, it was very dark. They would depend on the moonlight or follow their senses. Mama and her siblings were not overjoyed about this. However, it was part of their lives, so they did it.

Fortunately, Lime Tree Garden School was only about a mile from their home. In fact, it was close enough that they could see it from the house, which was on a slight gradient. Although it shouldn't have taken Mama and her siblings more than 20 minutes to walk to school, the journey often took longer as the children played around as they travelled!

Granny stayed home and would have their lunches ready for when Mama and her siblings came home at lunchtime. My cousin would tell the stories of how Granny and the other ladies of the neighbourhood would sit outside the yard around "stone heaps." These ladies would break the rocks into small stones for the Bauxite company. The morning would be spent having a good old chit chat about things happening in the district and beyond. This was their "news hour." As soon as they heard the school bell ring, they would all scatter, racing to get something ready for the children to eat before going back to school. Be mindful, this was not a situation where one went to the refrigerator and grabbed something to make sandwiches or a quick snack!

No, wood fires had to be made, pots put on, and food prepared. Ah! That was part of life for Mama and her siblings. Not just them, but the other children of the neighbourhood would have had the same experiences.

Mama's parents, as I understand, weren't wealthy in the sense of having a lot of money. They had several acres of farming land. Some of this land remains in the family today. They lived off the produce of the land through the sale of the ground provision or the animals.

Their home sounded happy. Although there were 13 children (Grand-dad had two children previously who did not live in that home). They all, with Granny and Grandpa lived in a tiny house consisting of three rooms, an outside toilet (latrine), and an area used as a bathroom. The kitchen was off the main building, and there was an area at the back where washing was done. They didn't have running water and had to get water from the tank. This seemed standard for the times in rural Jamaica.

Mama's childhood home

Mama and her sibling enjoyed each other's company. In the evenings, before going to bed, they would sit out on the "barbeque" —unlike the common term, this is a huge square of concrete where provisions like pimento, coffee, sorrel and such would be put out to dry.

OVERCOMING

Moonlit nights were their favourite; they would share "duppy" (malicious spirits) stories and old-time stories. Although these tales would often leave them feeling afraid and having bad dreams. At other times, they would play games such as hide and seek, playing with their shadows, playing with stones in a circle while singing to their hearts' content: "go dung a Manuel Road — gal an boy fe bruk rock stone…" That was fun!

Growing up, church was a big part of their lives. Sunday school and whatever activities being held at the church would be a community event. So church became integral to their upbringing.

One of my uncles often refers to a time when Mama was protecting one of her siblings from a bully. As she was beating up the perpetrator, he fell over the "gully bank" (side of the mound of the ground). His parents came to Mama's home the following day saying, "Ayia, a prison yu a go mi chile, a prison yu a go." I'm not sure what the response was, but knowing my gran, they would have left her property flying. That was the end of that prison sentence!

What Mama's aspirations and dreams were as a child is hard to say. Children living in those days were mainly just getting on with what life offered. They had a happy home, a mama and dad, and each other. There was always food to eat and plenty of it. Even if the meat was rationed, Granny would always rustle up something. She was such a good cook! Even now, as I remember some of the food prepared by my gran, especially the "bush cabbage," hmm, I begin to salivate!

OVERCOMING

Life in Maverley and surrounding Kingston areas (1960–1970)

I lived with my grandparents in the early years of my life. Therefore, my earliest memories of my mother were of living in a one-bedroom house in an area called Maverley in Kingston. I was about 5 years old. Our family then consisted of five children ranging from 1 to 6 years of age.

To my knowledge, Mama didn't have much formal education. This was a fairly standard situation for kids living in the rural areas. Education beyond elementary school was a luxury, and many of the poor families just couldn't afford to continue educating their children. This meant that there were a limited number of job opportunities available to young women, but Mama was prepared to do whatever it took to feed and clothe her children. Our father was not around. He had left and gone off to England, leaving her with their five children. Mama often said, "I hoped this was for a better life for us as a family!" However, this was not to be. Actually, our father had met and married another woman shortly before going off to England. Mama was not privy to this. Father later divorced and remained with another woman he met in England; they were married up until his passing.

Mama had to take in washing and do other domestic chores for money. Looking back, this must have been a very hard job for her. I remember laundry days, normally Thursday and Friday nights, folding sheets in the middle of the night with Mama. This was like a ritual. We would each hold an end of the sheet, fold and stretch its width, length, and then diagonally. This would continue until all the surfaces of the sheet were ironed. It was tedious work but provided great satisfaction when completed. They smelt so fresh and looked so crisp when they were neatly stacked.

I have been reminded by my sister that Mama also worked at a clothing factory, possibly putting trimming on finished garments. My sister remembers her bringing home her tools — shears, scissors, thimble, large spools of thread, etc. As children, we did not see that side of her life. We just knew we did not have many things, and food was scarce in our house. But it was the same for many of our neighbours, so it wasn't a huge hardship for us. The only difference is they had a dad living with them, and we did not.

OVERCOMING

We did have a few of our uncles come to stay every so often. One of our uncles lived with us during his training to be a police officer. That was great fun. He worked at a bakery prior to commencing his training, and he always brought us goodies from work. We were very happy to have him home with us. He was more like a big brother. It must have also been good for Mama to have another adult at home she could depend on. That must have been a relief and comfort to her.

We were happy and always well-presented when going to school or church, even if it was just the one suit — our Sunday best — or one uniform for school. We girls always had our hair nicely combed and tied with ribbons.

From an early age, we attended Sunday School regularly, although, at that point, Mama herself didn't go to church, she ensured we went. At the end of communion at church, we were given the bread that wasn't eaten to take home!

My mother had few friends at that time. However, her one special friend was Miss Gloria; they seemed to share everything, and I mean everything.

Sundays were good days. Mama would get us all dressed up, and we'd go for a "walk out" in the park. It wasn't far from our house, and it definitely wasn't fancy, but it made us feel special to be out as a family. We would see other friends at the park, and sometimes family members who came to visit would accompany us. We'd play games such as ring around the roses, hide and seek in the maze, or catch. Sometimes, we'd pick some of the flowers (and pray the park attendant didn't catch us!) and pretend we were princes and princesses. Often we just sat on the grass and chatted, making up stories. Mama would then get us fudge, icicles or a packet of peanuts, depending on what she could afford. We would then take the leisurely walk back home before it got dark.

We were oblivious to what our poor Mama must have been going through to raise us. However, there's no denying that times were tough. Groceries were often purchased with the promise of payment. However, days at our home at Kempton Avenue in Maverley did not seem to be as bad as the later years in Kingston.

My sister Charmaine (right) and me

Sunday also meant dessert after dinner. It was usually only jelly — no ice cream — but we all looked forward to the treat.

On a good week, when we had cow foot for dinner, there was also "cow foot jelly." This was the juice from the stew, sweetened and chilled. Mmmm, nice!

Mama was so innovative. She made the most of her limited resources to ensure her children were loved and cared for. I've been reminded of market days on Saturday. Mama would make the journey from Maverley to downtown Kingston to the Coronation market, maybe a 10-mile journey. Sometimes on her bicycle — a pedal bike — other times on the bus when she would take one of the boys with her. Whichever way she travelled, she would get a variety of fruits and vegetables and other ground provisions. Saturday soup was standard.

The most interesting thing was how Mama would balance that huge basket with all the food and vegetables on her head, especially on her pedal bike, maneuvering through the busy, dangerous streets of Kingston. Amazing!

Any of you, my readers, who live, have lived or visited Kingston and travelled these roads will have an idea of what I am talking about.

Mama was probably about 5'6 tall. As a child, she seemed to me like a giant. She really had a presence. Once, during a visit to England from

America, I took her into the Birmingham City Centre to do some shopping. I showed her where to catch the bus home, as I had to carry on to work. She must have wandered away or just became disorientated. For whatever reason, she just could not find the correct bus stop. So, in the middle of Birmingham City Centre, she stomped her foot and her walking stick and shouted, "Will someone please tell me where the bus stop is?" I understand that the whole of Birmingham City Centre stood still; everyone came forward to help her then.

Mama was a very strict woman, a disciplinarian. She would punish first and ask questions later. As kids, we hated that, saying, "It's not fair!" as we would often get an unnecessary whooping for something we did not do. Whenever we were acting up or getting out of line, Mama just had to clear her throat — as soon as we heard that specific sound, we knew to behave ourselves.

Her being such a disciplinarian stemmed from deep in her own past. The well-known story is told of the day her mother got married. Her dad "whipped" her, saying, "Manners is the way!" Who knows where that came from! I guess it's a generational thing, perhaps from the experience of slavery days.

Once, while at primary school, we experienced an episode of torrential rain. While we were walking home from school with friends, Mama wrapped herself in a plastic bag and headed to the school to meet us and to escort us home safely. She knew that all the water could flow quickly and pull someone off their feet and drag them away. We had gone home a different way, wading in the water, having fun, unaware of the dangers. Mama arrived home before us, and when we got home, the whooping started. There was no point trying to explain. She came to get us, and we chose to follow friends. We paid for our decision. Argument done!

We lived on Kempton Avenue for about five years. Life was not too bad then, but it took a downward spiral after moving from that house. We seemed to be forever moving; it felt like every month.

Let me clarify to you, my readers. Moving house in JA, especially for the poorer people, is not as straightforward as some may understand. Moving house was traumatic. There's no government help; people just have to get on the best they can with whatever they have. God and a good friend. And that's the category we were in.

We lived in the surrounding areas of Kingston. Although she was working with a shoe-string budget, Mama never rented in shanty, tenement, or ghetto areas. We always lived in respectable neighbourhoods. The lodgings were small, but the safety of her children (especially her girls) was her main focus. Her children's lives were to be preserved at all costs.

We moved regularly, sometimes in the rain, damaging or completely ruining what little furniture we had. My sister remembers her friends often saying, "Uno move again? Uno can move, eh!" Mama tried, but she couldn't shield us from everything.

We once lived in a property that was owned by a friend's husband. The rent must have been due and poor Mama was not able to find it. The landlord had the bailiffs in. One morning while we were having our breakfast before going off to school, the bailiffs came in, put our bowls on the floor, and took our dining table away. It wasn't fancy, but it was ours, something we were really proud to own. And just like that, it was gone. I remembered when it first arrived at our home at Kempton Ave. We were so proud and happy; elated: we now had a dining table! No more sitting on the floor or the bed to have our meals. Now with it taken away, we were back to where we were, sitting on the floor or bed to eat. *That hurt!* Having our dining table taken away like that must have been a deep hurt for Mama. I know that as kids, we were very sad; for her, it must have been devastating. I must say, however, I never saw our mother cry. Who was she going to cry to? Us children?

Just before her passing, I asked her: "Why did we have to move so regularly?"

"I could find the first month's rent to move in, but by the time the next month was due, hard times hit again," she told me. That was the sum total of Mama's life at that time. However, she never gave up. She kept going, trusting that better days would come. And they did, eventually. Thanks be to God.

Looking back now, I regret not asking, questioning, digging up more about her life when we were kids. I feel now there is so much of my mother's life I'm not aware of or have even taken for granted.

OVERCOMING

MAKING ENDS MEET

We were all involved in helping Mama get enough money for food and rent. When there were parties or dances held in the community over the weekend, my brothers would go early the next morning to pick up the empty drink bottles and bring them home. Actually, whenever one of us saw an empty glass bottle, we would pick it up and take it home to add to the collection, adding value to the stock. When we had a substantial amount, the bottles were then sold back to the store, which would return them to the drinks manufacturer to be used again.

Field trips, community events, school activities — we were never left out. Mama would always find a way for us to be involved. My older sister was always put forward for festivals or other school activities. At these events, it was mandatory to wear the school's uniform. The teacher reminded them the day before: "See you in the morning looking smart. Be ready for the performance."

Unfortunately, neither of my sister's two uniforms were smart. One was washed out, and the other was threadbare from the excessive washing and ironing. For a young child, her thoughts were, "Lawd, a wha mi a go do?"

Mama had a plan, though. When my sister got home from school, to her amazement, hanging on the clothesline was a "brand new" uniform!

"How did you manage that?" she asked.

Mama had bought dye and dyed the washed-out uniform, making it look brand new again! My sister said she looked just as smart as the other children. That was *Mama*. She would do whatever it took so that her children never felt less than everyone else.

While we were still quite young, Mama had an opportunity to travel to the United States of America. There was this sponsorship programme going, which she must have enrolled in. As my sister says, Mama had received all the forms and paperwork and was in the process of completing them, then decided against the move. She was in a desperate situation, and some might have said, "This is a Godsend." Mama, however, refused to leave us. Who would look after five children and care for them without the certainty of any financial assistance? It would have been difficult to have anyone to care for us without having to split us up. That she didn't want; having us to be passed from home to home. Her children were not pets to be handed out. So she endured her struggles.

I keenly remember one incident, not long after giving birth to our baby brother, her wash belly (as we call the last child). She took me with her to downtown Kingston to do some shopping. We were about ready to return home when she must have remembered something she needed. She left me — I was probably about 13 years old — at the bus stop with the shopping, saying, "Wait here for me."

I do not know what happened or what she was thinking. On her return, she could not find me. I guess the place was so crowded with "Higglers" (peddlers) and all sorts. She almost went off her head. I was eventually found, about two hours later, at the very place she had left me. This is after she had gone home and returned to the city looking for me. Don't ask how that happened! Mama seemed to have aged with worry over that period.

You know, thinking about that incident and how I felt while being in that crowded city centre, alone, it occurs to me that I wasn't worried and surely didn't panic. I was at peace with myself, knowing that my mother would soon show up. In fact, whenever I visited my grandmother's house, she would cover me with a blessing, saying, "Touch not the LORD's anointed." She repeated this over and over. I didn't give it much thought then, but I guess I have been protected from many dangers, even then!

You may think I am romanticising my mother's life, but I assure you that I'm not. Her life was tough and made her very harsh at times. Suffice to say, I did not always feel this affectionate towards my mother. However, as I grew up and began to see life for what it is, raising my own children, I began to appreciate and ponder on her life. How did she do it, overcoming all these struggles and challenges?

AN EMOTIONAL TOLL

Thinking about her life, Mama must have experienced times of depression, despair, discouragement, frustration, oppression, and just being emotionally and psychologically bankrupt.

"Mama never smiled," my sister said to me recently. I think she may have been experiencing these emotions and had no one to share them with, no outlet. Whenever she was with her friend Miss Gloria, especially when engrossed in her favourite television programmes ("Perry Mason," "The Fugitive," and "Dr Kildare"), they would laugh. In fact, that was about all the entertainment she had at the time. Later on in life, with her church family and work colleagues, she was much lighter. She laughed more then.

Mama and her church sisters

PSYCHOLOGICAL BANKRUPTCY

I cannot remember Mama ever giving us a hug or saying that she loved us. None of us, though, has suffered any ill effects from this lack of expression, nor do we hold this against her.

Actually, this seems to be a very West Indian thing.

Our parents did not have this experience, so this may not be seen as a priority. Furthermore, Mama was under pressure, struggling to bring up five small children single-handedly without a steady job. Her upbringing didn't lend itself to that sort of affection. Survival was the name of the game. We knew we were all loved and well taken care of. For us, as children growing up, we felt love and knew Mama was doing the best she could under the circumstances. We appreciate the solid morals and values based on Bible principles with which we were brought up.

Her children are well-balanced, respectable, upstanding members of the societies in which they live. This speaks of her strong character, determination, and courage. Mama was a force to contend with. She knew where her strength came from: her God! She invested all she had in her children, often sacrificing herself in the process. When your life has a strong purpose, you push past your pain to fulfil it. Mama's purpose was to protect and preserve her children's lives.

One of Mama's rituals, as we got older, was to sit us down every New Year's eve and enquire of us individually, "What is your will and pleasure for the coming year?" To which she would expect to hear some goals we had set. Often these responses were quiet vague.

Mother was a godly woman, although not always. She was not perfect. There was a period, around this time, a certain family took a "real set," antagonising us, cussing us, wreaking havoc in our lives. Mama would cuss them back in return. My sister said she would often join in the cussing, to which Mama would tell her to "go si dung, lef big people argument." Once, when she'd had enough of this, she made a scarecrow using a mop head and placed it between the two houses, so when they were cursing, they would speak to the mop scarecrow. When that didn't work, she had to get down "real dirty." I can say, after that, we lived in peace and were never bothered by that family again.

I am sure whenever she remembered that incident, she cringed!

Part Two

THE MOVE TO PORTMORE (1970–1989)

Jabez cried out to God, "Oh that you would bless me and enlarge my territory; …" And God granted his request. (1Chronicles 4:10)

As the song goes, "Things can only get better."

Yes! Mama found favour with God. She learned of a new housing scheme opening up outside of Kingston. A housing developer bought an area of cane fields and created a low-cost housing scheme.

Our baby brother's father was working with the developers as a construction worker. He made the necessary contacts and provided Mama with the information and possibly financial resources to facilitate this move. The process seemed to have been very efficient and smooth. From the time of her being aware of the possibility of moving to the actual move, the time seemed no more than probably a couple of months.

We moved to Independence City in March 1970. This became our home for a long time, up until I left for England in 1989. No more moving house! God, You are so good. You promise never to leave or forsake us. You promise to provide. Thank You, Lord.

At the time of us moving to this area, it was one small community. Now the area is vastly developed with numerous communities and is known as part of the Portmore Area.

We had a whole house to ourselves — two bedrooms, a kitchen, a bathroom, living room, veranda, carport (garage), and lots of space for a garden. Mama, at one time, planted peanuts — yes, peanuts — in the front garden. Imagine that, eh!

My brother and sister both say that if they were to make an educated guess, Mama would have liked to be a farmer. Not because her father was one, but because of the way she gravitated towards the soil. She was very "green-fingered." Everything she planted grew to great proportions. There was a time, at our home in Independence City, when every plot of soil was always cultivated with whatever Mama could find to plant. My sister once said to her, "Mama, everyone else has flowers in their garden. Why do we have to have vegetables?!" Mama's response was, "Yu can eat flowers?" That put paid to the questioning.

We did eventually have flowers/plants in our garden. Mama's front garden was a beauty. She had Crotons, different species, Lilies, Joseph Coat, and Fern to name a few. She would spend hours both morning and evenings watering and caring for her plants.

The property at Independence City was rented; the owners were a very good and generous family who didn't put any pressure on us. Our brother's dad, I believed, would have helped Mama with the rent. He didn't actually live with us permanently; he visited regularly as part of supporting his child, our baby brother, who we loved so much; we all spoiled him. We never did get the opportunity to buy this property. I was very sad, on one of my visits home, to hear the property was sold. There was quite an attachment to that house. Not only due to the fact that we were the first to occupy it from new but because some of the grandchildren — four — were born and had their early years in that home, *Aah!*

I don't recall what work Mama did for the first couple of years living in our new home, but I do know that she still faced financial challenges. Three of us kids had to travel back into Kingston for school every day. The journey was long, and we would leave home early in the mornings.

Travelling to Kingston for school from our home in Independence City, if we had our own transport, would be about an hour's journey. However, travelling as we had to — changing vehicles and not knowing whether we would get on a bus — took us longer, maybe close to two hours. We would leave home at about 6 a.m. Our baby brother's dad had arranged for a van driver who would pick him up from the house while he was there to get us in the mornings. That was half of the journey covered. For the rest of the journey, we depended on God's mercy.

There were times — many, many times — when Mama was unable to find lunch money or bus fare for us to get to and from school. We would get there by God's grace, hitchhiking. A faithful van driver was always ready and willing to pick us up whenever he saw us. And he didn't do it just for us. There were always a few other youngsters in need of a ride. We were not able to pay the fare, and he knew that.

Mama had initiative to the max. Living in Independence City, she started her own business. The area was still being developed, and there was a dearth of infrastructure. As more families moved in, the need for child care grew. So Mama got to work. She and my older sister, who by now had finished school, opened a nursery (day care) and nursery school, using the knowledge and experience she gained from caring for her siblings, her own children and children of friends and families.

Our home had lots of yard space, including a veranda, but even with all this space, she couldn't accommodate all of the babies whose parents wanted to make use of her services. After a while, the day nursery extended into an infant school. This eventually became an established registered school, the Independence City Basic School. (*G'wan*, Mama, you are on your way!)

My mother and my sister enrolled in a teacher's training programme, where they were able to work and study at the same time. They attended workshops in the evenings, as well as weekend tutorial sessions and fortnightly sessions during the summer holidays. Both Mama and my sister earned a Level 3 certificate in Early Childhood Education.

Over the next few years, the establishment outgrew the property. By this time, however, there was a community and function centre being built. An application was submitted requesting permission to use the centre to house the basic school during the daytime. As there were no other such facilities in the area at that time, and this request served the needs of the community, there was no objection. Permission granted. Great! It did mean that the nursery had to close, and although the parents were sad about it, they made alternative plans.

The school was rehoused in the community centre, where it fulfilled the needs of the community for a very, very long time — from 1973 to 2005. To facilitate this, Mama had to have furniture made. Benches, desks, chairs, as well as chalkboards and cupboards for storing teaching materials and equipment. Mama was now an employer, as she needed teachers and assistant teachers. Apart from the increasing number of students, their varied ages required appropriate staffing. Mama was now not only an employer but also the Principal/ Headteacher of this school.

Mama's hard work and ingenuity made her a pillar of the community. In time, the Independence City Basic School became a recognised institution by the Ministry of Education. Almost all the young people of the community transitioned from this school on to their further education. Their foundation learning started right there. For that, many parents and even the young people themselves are grateful. One of the many events attesting to this fact is, at her homegoing service in New York, roughly sixty per cent of the people there were some of the young people who had gone through her school. They spoke highly of the input "Madda" had made in their lives.

If you walk through Independence City now and mention the name Miss Lewis or Madda, someone is bound to know her or of her. The school was a huge success. Not only was it her livelihood, but it also offered effective caring, nurturing, educational grounding and development for young people, and was a place of employment for many.

Harry T. Moore, one of the original American civil rights activists (possibly quoting Theodore Roosevelt), once stated, "What a man does for himself dies with him, but what he does for his community lives forever!" (Harry T. Moore, 1951). So true. After Mama left Jamaica for America in 1989, my sister kept the Independence City Basic School running for many years. The school closed in 2005. The end of an era.

The building housing the school was built and owned by an organization known as the Urban Development Corporation (UDC). This was a community project responsible for the care and maintenance of the building. There was no charge for the use of the building. It was, however, the responsibility of those using the premises to keep it clean and report any need for repair. Any major work needed would be undertaken by the UDC.

Unfortunately, due to ill repair of the building and poor health issues experienced by the staff, the school is now permanently closed. The end of a chapter, yet the memories live on. The interesting thing is, this community centre and its surrounding grounds are in the centre of the community. Every direction you go, you pass it!

FINDING FAITH IN CHRIST

When we moved to Independence City, another family was living on our street — a grandmother and her grandchildren. She was a member of a church from the Kingston area, and she invited one of the ministers to hold Bible study in her living room. At the first meeting, it was just Granny, as we called her, her granddaughter, Mama, myself and one other neighbour in attendance. This soon became a weekly meeting, and very soon, the gathering outgrew Granny's living room. After a while, even the veranda, carport and yard were overflowing. Looking back, we were witnessing the mighty hand of God gathering people hungry for His word and for Him. Amos 8:11, the LORD declares, "I will send a famine on the land — not a famine of bread, nor a thirst for water, but hearing the words of the LORD." It still amazes me!

The church grew and grew, pastored by a variety of pastors. A visionary pastor saw the need and encouraged the congregation to acquire land and construct a building to host God's people. In May 1979, we held the ground-breaking ceremony for the Portmore Church of Christ, which we remain in contact with. Whenever I visit Jamaica, that's my home church.

By this time, Mama had accepted Christ as her Lord and Saviour. She had fully committed her life to walking in Christian love and faith. Life was not always easy; she still faced many challenges. One of her major challenges was that she used to curse. She cursed a lot. She would take no nonsense from anyone. It was wonderful to see the transformation, over a period of time, of what God is able to do with a surrendered heart.

The Bible does tell us that it is not always going to be all good. Christ told His disciples: "In this life, there will be many troubles ... but don't worry, I have overcome" (John 16:33); so we will overcome.

Mama was now not only the proprietor of her own business, headteacher of a school with a complement of staff; she was also a foundation and an active member of a church that is still functioning today. She was part of the women's ministry, planning and executing activities and events. She was a member of the choir, which performed at various events in addition to the worship services.

OVERCOMING

Mama loved to sing. You would hear her singing as she worked. One of her favourite songs was "What a friend we have in Jesus." She also loved reading. I can't say I saw her reading novels; however, she spent much time reading her Bible and the newspaper, not to mention the preparatory work for her school lesson plans.

Up to the time of Mama's passing in 2011, I was the only one of her children who followed "the way." One of my sisters has since accepted Christ, being baptised and walking in His love. My prayer continues for the rest of my family. I stand on the words of Joshua 24:15 "... as for me and my house, we will serve the Lord." So I pray!

Every Sunday morning, Mama would get us up so early, while it was still dark outside, for prayer, devotion, and worship. I can tell you a 5 a.m. wake-up call on a Sunday morning did not go down well with my siblings. But there was no use fighting it. Mama had decided, and that was that! There would be scripture readings, songs, and prayers. Oftentimes, our hearts were not in it; we just wanted to go back to bed. To our mother, this time was an investment in her children's spiritual welfare. As far as she was concerned, this was not going to be compromised. This continued even after she was married and lived next door with her husband.

HER MARRIAGE

Mama gave us kids the best she could afford in this new environment. We were older now — I was about 16 years old, so our ages ranged from about 6 to 17. Now we the older ones were able to do chores around the house — cooking, keeping the house tidy, assisting with preparing meals — which took some of the pressure off of her. In fact, if I remember clearly, most of the household chores were undertaken by myself, especially the cooking.

Mama was a good cook, a very good cook. She just took so long; it felt like we waited forever to have our evening meals. That's maybe why I ended up taking on most of the cooking. She taught me well how to cook. She was a good teacher!

Mama enjoyed her food, so it must have been a great challenge and disgusting to her in later years when she became ill and had to have her food liquidized. Oh, so sad!

Oranges were one of her favourite fruits. She loved big and juicy oranges; the bigger, the better. She liked the ones we call "navel oranges." I recall I had gone shopping and bought some; they were not the sizes she was used to having. She never ate one of them. When I enquired why, her response was, "Dem ya too likle." *Ha!*

Living next door to us was a single man who took a fancy to our mother. They courted for a short while as she wasn't prepared to live with him out of marriage. This went against her faith and her walk with Christ. They got married in November 1973. The wedding wasn't a grand affair. I was about 16 years old and was tasked, with the help of a cousin, to do the cooking for the occasion. *Ha!* It was mainly our family, as her husband did not have many, only a sister, as I recall.

Getting married was another challenge Mama had to face. Her husband was a divorcee, and getting remarried was something many of the church's congregants, not to mention our pastor, deemed as going against the word of God. She had to search really hard to find a pastor of her faith to perform the ceremony. Through her relentless faith, one pastor was prepared to bless their union. Mama moved in with her husband, and I wish I could say that they lived happily ever after, but it wasn't so.

The wedding day was a lovely sunny day, as we have in Jamaica. My siblings remember it being a morning wedding. Mama, wearing a traditional white dress, and her husband went off to the church / register office. On their return, breakfast, consisting of ackee and saltfish with fried dumplings, was served. The afternoon was a big party, a celebration with "food galore," as my sister put it. We served curry goat, rice, vegetables and salad, cake and lots of drinks. This occasion was a really big thing for us, as we were never before able to afford such extravagance. This didn't appear to be a traditional wedding, as we children didn't actually attend the wedding ceremony. Some of Mama's husband's friends and a few of the neighbours came over to celebrate the occasion with us.

We wanted so much to see our mother happy. We were so happy for her and about her marriage. We hoped she would finally get a shot at being looked after, and cared for, as she deserved. The marriage was a rocky one, to say the least. Her husband was okay, but some of his ways were very unbecoming. I guess living in the circle of his work environment caused him to be somewhat "coarse." He had been living this way for a long time, almost all his adult life, and he wasn't a young man at that point. He was probably not what she hoped for. Nevertheless, she stayed married to him to the very end.

Uncle Robbie, as we called Mama's husband, owned the property next door. He lived alone, and, as already mentioned, he was divorced. He had no children of his own that we were aware of. He traded wares — pots, pans, pails, washbowls, brooms and such like. He traded his wares in the heart of Downtown Kingston (Spanish Town Road), a really rough part of town.

Him marrying Mama with six children? Not sure what his thoughts were. He was, however, good to us, except to our youngest brother, he wasn't very kind to him, especially as he got older. We loved our baby brother so much. He was dear to all our hearts. He was never abusive to us, more so when the grandchildren came along; he adored them. Treated them as his own special prizes. No one could say anything about them, and there wasn't anything too good for him to give them. They, in return, expressed that same love and affection towards their uncle Robbie.

The same affection, however, was not shown to Mama. "Why do you put up with this?" I asked several times when things were bad. I cannot even remember her response. Oh, what we do for the sake of love! Was it love, though, or commitment?

Thinking about it, I wonder why they got married. Was it for love, companionship, financial stability, security…? I guess we'll never know. Along the street we lived in were approximately 50 homes. Every home had families consisting of married couples. Until Mama married, only two or three, Mama included, were single-parent households! Did Mama secretly felt left out? Who knows!

Don't get me wrong, the marriage was not all bad. Uncle Robbie eventually gave his life to Christ, was baptised, and they followed God together. Those were good times. Bless his soul, may he rest in peace.

By now, we were in a unique position of occupying two homes. Mama and her husband were next door, while we had the run of our original home. I wish! Just because she didn't live in the house did not stop her from having jurisdiction over what went on in the house we children lived in. She was the one who paid the upkeep for that property. Mama would do her rounds, checking that all our chores were completed, and we were all in bed, doors locked, by 10 p.m. at the latest. She would even come over in the middle of the night to check we were all still in bed.

My older sister had the habit of sneaking out, especially on a Saturday night, after Mama had done her nightly rounds. She would go off to dances and parties with her boyfriend. Somehow Mama got wind of this, and oftentimes my sister would come home to find her sitting, waiting with some implements ready to administer a whooping. But it never stopped my sister. She loved her partying as much, I suspect, as she loved her boyfriend, who became her husband, lifelong partner, and friend. May he also rest in eternal peace.

You can never keep a good woman down!

Mama was a very hardworking, industrious, independent, caring, kind, dedicated, hospitable woman. She was faithful to her church, her children, her family, and her community. Our friends often said how lovely our mother was.

"You can say that. You don't have to live with her!" was our standard response.

In retrospect, I believe that often her harsh treatment was how she tried to protect us from the challenges she herself had experienced in those earlier years of her life. It sounds crazy, but at the heart of all this, our psychological, social, and spiritual welfare were her priority.

THE PROVERBS 31 WOMAN

Mama was a fiercely independent woman, and although she was now a married woman, she would never cause her or her children to be a financial burden to anyone, so she often supplemented her earnings by trading wares. She would travel to places such as Panama, Curacao and Haiti to buy clothing, underwear, footwear, bedding and houseware — whatever she could make a profit on. She would sell to the community throughout the year, and in the run-up to Christmas, she would invest in a stall in downtown Kingston in King Street. Often, business was good, sometimes not so good. *Hey!*

OVERCOMING

God is our provider. He kept her through the storm.

We enjoyed being in downtown Kingston during the Christmas period, sometimes all night. Christmas Eve was known as "Grand Market." It's as if every single person was out in town. There was a real buzz. Such excitement, carol-singing, sounds of children blowing fefe whistles and other toys on sale, music playing. It was like a carnival atmosphere. The grandchildren thought it was great fun being pushed around on the "handcart" that was used to transport goods, and being in the thick of this hustle and bustle. It was great!

West Indian/Caribbean readers may be familiar with the concept of "pardner" — a weekly collection of funds from a community of people. A banker collects and pays out the funds weekly. This was done on trust. Mama often ran pardner and was let down so often. For the sake of the few trustworthy participants, though, she would often restart the programme. Sacrificing for the good of the few! This makes no sense, but that is just who Mama was.

Although we were not young children who needed intense care and attention, there were other needs that Mama felt were her responsibility, as a mother, to fulfil. Our education was paramount. She was fanatical about us getting a proper education, refusing to compromise on quality. First-hand experience of receiving only a basic education made her determined that none of us be left to the "macy" of the world, one of our Jamaican sayings. We all received secondary education, and three of us went on to high school and two to university.

In Jamaica, schooling starts with basic school (usually ages 3 to 6), attending daily from 9 a.m. to 3 p.m. Then, at age 6, children move on to an all-age school, where they remain until age 15. At age 11, pupils are encouraged to "sit" the Common Entrance Examination and move on to High School. It is not uncommon for parents to pay for extra tuition in order for their child to do well in these exams. I, however, was not successful at my Common Entrance exam; I used up all the attempts available to me. There was, however, another exam allowed — the Grade Nine Achievement test — at which my brother and I were successful. He went to a Technical College while I went to a high school, Wolmers High School for Girls. One brother, who had got to the position of Attorney General, was offered a scholarship, which took him to the University of the West Indies, Mona Campus, then to Russia, where he spent about seven years studying International Law. In fact, he was there at the time of the Chernobyl disaster in 1986. Those were some heart-wrenching times for our family, as news about him was slow to come forth.

Not bad achievements for the kids who were probably the poorest on the block, without a daddy. Thanks, Mama, you were one of a kind.

FAMILIES VISITING FROM ABROAD

Often we had families visiting from abroad, mainly our British relatives — aunts, uncles, cousins. They often stayed at our house. No one was ever turned away, no matter how many people there were. There was always room; we made room.

I have come to hear stories of families here in the UK not looking forward to visiting their families in Jamaica because of the attitude of constant expectancy. Their Jamaican relatives were always "gimme, gimme, gimme" and showed very little appreciation for the things they received. Thankfully, I can say not so with our family. Mama's brothers and sisters may or may not have known of her struggles, but whenever they visited, comfort and welcome were always maxed out. We were always happy and excited when our families came to visit. One uncle who visited from England exclaimed that we were rich! Why? Because we had a "helper" — a maid — at home. "Only rich people in England can afford to have a maid," he told us.

Having the nursery and the infant school, we needed someone to help out with the chores, mainly washing, cleaning and general tidying up after all the babies. And we weren't alone. Having a helper or day worker was a very common practice in the community. This not only helps the householder but also provides an earning for someone, a dignified help to someone less fortunate.

We looked forward to having our family from abroad visit. During the summer of 1975, our aunt, her husband, and their three children visited. The adults stayed in the country, while our cousins stayed with us. That was great fun. We did everything together, and we loved introducing them to our friends and our community. They loved it, too. For two of them, it was their one and only trip to Jamaica. I give God thanks that we were part of that experience.

Me with my sister Charmaine(left) and our cousin Julia (right)

The Bible tells us we should love each other deeply, as well as offer and practice hospitality. This was one of Mama's best traits. One

Christmas holiday, one of her brothers and his wife visited from America. They stayed with my aunt's family, but they visited us on Boxing Day (26th December).

Now, most Jamaicans don't celebrate Christmas and Boxing Day the same way as the British and the Americans do. When we were younger, there was not much difference from one day to the next, as money was scarce. Even as life improved financially, Christmas dinner never really happened in our house. We had a huge breakfast (ackee and saltfish, huge slices of hard dough bread, roast ham, washed down with chocolate tea), *yum yum*. Throughout the day, we would visit friends and neighbours, enjoying Jamaican rum cake, sorrel drink, and slices of ham.

On Boxing Day, we would have a "spread," and what a spread indeed. Rice and peas, at least three different types of meat, salad, steamed veg, fried dumplings, fried plantains, rum cake, sorrel drink, rum punch. It was an extravagance that we could usually only afford once a year.

So, my uncle and aunt came to visit on Boxing Day. And my, was she surprised, and very impressed. For years, she talked about how well she was received that day. Mama never saw it as a big deal. She was just doing what she did best — welcoming guests with the very best she had. Nothing was too good for her to give to her family. Anyone who visited got only the best.

As a believer in God, Mama exemplified generosity throughout her life. It is said that giving is the loftiest level of living. Generous people focus their time and effort on what they can give others, not what they can get from them. This was Mama's attitude. No matter how little she had, she always asked, "What can I give?" It is not what you have that matters; it is what you do with what you have. There is a famous saying by Winston Churchill, "We make a living by what we get, but we make a life by what we give." I guess this attitude of giving was learnt from her parents. Our gran would almost give what she didn't have. Kids were known to stop off at her house, and even if it was simply a "sugar lump," they would leave with something.

Reflecting on Mama's life, she lived by this principle daily. One of her nephews was heard to say that he loved visiting Auntie Dell, as he knew she would always have a coin to put in his hand, no matter the value. What a testimony!

Mama's sister from the country, and our cousins would come to stay with us. Whatever the reason, she needed to be away from her home for a break. Mama always accommodated them and made them feel not just welcome but comfortable, too.

You know, having access to both homes was a godsend, for there was always "room at the inn." I sometimes wonder if Mama ever wished that she had a refuge, somewhere to go when life got too hard. But she knew God to be her refuge and strength, a present help in times of trouble. She no doubt knew that though she may be forsaken by all others; families, her children's father...her God would never forsake her. Even going through the valley overshadowed with death, debt, lack, loneliness, emptiness, and hungry children, she feared not! Why? She knew her God was with her. (Psalm 23:4)

THE GRANDCHILDREN

By this time, grandchildren were being born to Mama. Our older brother and sister, who were both brought up by family members, each had children. They visited regularly and would often stay with us.

OVERCOMING

Over a period of five years (1978–1982), Mama had six grandchildren. Four of them — my two and my youngest sister's two — were all born in the home at Independence City. Although my older sister lived in her own home, her two children were regularly at the home as they were all raised together, more or less. They slept together; they didn't care which of the homes they slept at, whether with Mama, or us, their parents. They ate together, played together and wore each other's clothes. These children were inseparable. There was always a jostle to see who would get on Mama's lap first. It was fascinating to watch. As children, we never had that experience.

Mama loved her grandchildren. These kids would get away with things we would have been given a whooping for. They had "softened" her. She was still very strict and had set moral standards. Sunday school was a must, and they enjoyed going, learning the songs, scripture texts and Bible stories. They all went to her school. It was during one of these pregnancies, I can't remember if it was mine or my youngest sister's, that Mama started having issues with her blood pressure.

Some of Mama's grandchildren

BEGINNINGS OF HEALTH CHALLENGES

During the mid-80s, Mama started having medical issues — hypertension, diabetes and painful joints, among others. She was never actually diagnosed with arthritis, but it was believed that this was the reason for her aching joints. Of all her complaints, this proved to be her most debilitating one. She was always in pain, which started with her knee, then her hip. I often massaged her joints with all-natural remedies just to help her to get through the day.

Mama would finish school around 2:30 p.m. After cleaning up and clearing away, she would be out of the building around 3 p.m. The 10 to 15-minute walk home would take her 60 to 90 minutes. This was partly because she stopped to talk with community members, but she also had to stop and rest her aching joints frequently. She struggled through the discomfort of painful joints without the help of pharmaceutical medication. She mainly depended on home remedies. Mama would try everything. Some gave relief, and some not so much. I often used to wonder: "Is this real, or is she making this up?" Honestly!

Aah, the amount of "rubbing" I gave Mama daily, especially at bedtime. I could be considered to be a physiotherapist, a masseur of natural remedies.

Not long after I moved to the UK, finishing work one morning, an excruciating pain shot up my right arm from the tip of my middle finger up to my shoulder. I thought of Mama and understood what she had been experiencing all those years. Sorry, Mama, for doubting you.

Mama would regularly go to a mineral bath in St. Thomas or one of the surrounding areas to have a soak. She enjoyed that, and it did give her some relief. She also loved to go to one of the many beaches that were close to our home to "sap" her joints with the seawater. Dunn's River

Waterfalls in the parish of St. Ann was another of her favourites, and she frequented it regularly.

Mama at Dunns River Falls

As I am aware, Mama was not officially diagnosed with arthritis. She knew her dad had "painful joints," and now she had it. Her philosophy was to just get on with life! The option of joint replacement was never mentioned, neither was it offered. In Jamaica, we do not have the facility of a National Healthcare System. Citizens have to pay for all their healthcare, and that can be very costly. Procedures of this calibre could work out very expensive; money which Mama didn't have. I know, though, if it had come to that, the funds would be made available somehow. God is our provider. He has promised that He'll provide for our needs. He had been doing so all her life; why would He bow out now?

DAD'S VISIT

Our father left Jamaica for England in the early 1960s on one of the ships carrying many West Indian and Caribbean natives who were invited to join the workforce in the "Motherland." He left Mama, a young woman without a stable income, with five young children. The story we believe he told her was that he was going to seek a better life for the whole family. He sent some sort of financial support for a couple of years until she sent proof of his children back in Jamaica. Our birth certificates allowed him to claim taxes for his dependent children, so the story goes. Mama said nothing was heard of him again. We grew up not knowing if our father was dead or alive.

I previously mentioned Mama not having a streak of "bad mind" (envy) about her. Here is what I mean. This man left her "flat on her face" with five children, and in all her struggles, she never ever said a negative word about him to us. He just was not talked about. I thought about him all the time, especially after one letter he wrote about how cold it was there. He had sent a doll for my sister, which we cherished. Other than that, *nothing*!

Around January or February 1984, I was in the front garden doing some work when I was approached by a young man. Honestly, I couldn't make sense of what he was saying, but eventually, I understood he was a cousin of ours on our father's side. He had come with a message that our father was coming to visit Jamaica and wanted to see us! "What? Come again! Mr Leslie Combrie is planning to visit Jamaica and wishes to come see us, his children he deserted for so many years? You gotta be kidding me!"

He assured me this was a fact and provided me with an address. In fact, it was the address we'd always known for him — our father — I took the address and bid him farewell. "Fuming" is an understatement for what I was feeling at that point. I can't really recall Mama's response to this news. I know my siblings became more irate than I was. How dare he! He'd left us for all those years without any contact, and now he wished to turn up with an address? He didn't have the decency to make the effort to write to us!

Anyway, after simmering for a month or so, I wrote to him and really told him exactly what we thought. At the end of the letter, I included our phone number and advised that if he still wished to make contact, he could do so. Nothing happened for a while; to be truthful, I didn't really expect anything from the way the letter was stated.

One afternoon, I was out in the garden with Mama again when we heard the phone ringing. I answered and heard a strange voice. When I inquired who it was, yes, you guessed it! It was our father. Shock, anger, hurt, pain, excitement all at once overtook me. This roller coaster of emotions stunned me into silence. I was speechless for a while. I eventually composed myself, and the barrage of "cussing" — not rude words, mind you — I was overwhelmed, and the contents of the letter and other things that were not said then, he received in full force. In fairness to him, he took the barrage of cussing without uttering a word. He remained silent throughout.

After purging myself of all this pent up pain and hurt, I composed myself, and we had a civil conversation that went on for roughly two hours. He then spoke with Mama and gave us his phone number, encouraging us to call him anytime, collect. That evening, nothing got done. My head was spinning. I had to contact the others to let them know of the new development. I passed on his number with the information received.

In the summer of 1984, our father visited Jamaica. This was not his first visit, we understood, but it was the one during which we were able to meet him. We had a reasonably good time, going to places of interest and spending time getting to know him. I had never seen him before. Maybe the younger ones had seen him before but they certainly didn't remember what he looked like. Our older sister would have known him before he left for England.

OVERCOMING

We had many questions that needed answering. We knew restitution wouldn't come in this one sitting, but this was a good place to start. Mama was always involved in this process, as this affected her life as much as it did ours. So, after a real shaky start, with some deep, radical questioning and painful revelations, I was able to commence the healing process. Matthew 6:12 tells us as we ask forgiveness, we need to forgive others. Forgiveness; that's where the healing begins. Because of the pain he had caused Mama, some of my siblings did not want to have anything to do with him before his passing.

Father did make subsequent visits to Jamaica, during which we briefly met up with him. His wife was not with him on this first visit. We did eventually meet her, though there was no interaction with her. Neither with Mama nor us. We were just introduced to her as his wife. It was a tense and uncomfortable moment, especially for our father. Something we learned on his first visit was that he was a man who didn't handle confrontation well.

Our mother loved — really loved — our father. She never said so, but just from the way she acted around him, I could tell she felt cheated.

She bore him five beautiful children, and he just walked away. Another woman might have shredded him to pieces, but not our mother. She was too dignified for that.

His visit did, however, cause a lot of upset between Mama and me. We were constantly arguing. Everything I did was a problem. Especially when I had been out with our father, the rest of my siblings and the grandchildren. Yes, I was going to spend what time I could with him. The father I thought was "dead" was there in our presence. This was a true work of God Himself.

I was still living at home; all the other siblings except my younger brother had left home by then and were raising their own families. I believe Mama felt deserted. He had turned up after so many years away and was receiving all this undeserved attention, almost like the younger brother in the parable of The Prodigal Son (Luke 15:11-32). She must have felt like the older brother! Despite all of her struggles and sacrifice, we were heaping attention on the man who had left her. It was only for the duration of his holiday, but that did not make it any easier for her to handle. All the hurt and anger that she had repressed for so long surfaced, and I bore the brunt of it.

Father kept in contact with us after his return to England. The next time my parents met was in December 1997. I had invited Mama over to England for my graduation after qualifying in my chosen profession. For some months leading up to my finals and graduation, there was not much conversation between my father and me. He did call me out of the blue, after a period of about six months, asking if he could come to see me for a visit. We had a terse conversation on the phone, but I let him know that he was always welcome at my home, no matter what.

After hanging up the call, it dawned on me that Mama would be there when he came to visit. We promised to keep it a secret. Mama was excited. It would be such a surprise when he arrived. I do not know who was more nervous when they finally met, him or her!

My dad, I came to understand, was a very private man, and as we'd noticed, he didn't take well to confrontation. Though this was a pleasant meeting, he was taken unawares; not expecting to see mother threw him off guard. Again, you could hear the nervousness in his voice. After the initial shaky start, they both relaxed and enjoyed the evening and each other's company.

Oh, it was so beautiful, just seeing them together. After they overcame the initial butterflies, they both relaxed, and we all had a truly beautiful afternoon. They chatted, laughed, ate, and drank. There was much to eat and drink. Dad returned to London that evening. Mama returned to the USA at the end of January 1998. After a short illness, my father died in May 1998.

I wondered what prompted Dad to request that visit. He was unwell; however, none of us knew of this illness. I remember opening the door to him, and before greeting him, I said, "You have lost some weight!" He responded with one of his nervous laughs. Dad was a well-built man, so I was surprised to see him so small then. It was after Mama's return to the USA that I was told of his illness.

Rest in peace, Dad!

OVERCOMING

Mama and Dad

Part three

LIFE IN THE USA

"To Him who is able to do exceedingly abundantly above all that we ask or think, according to the power that works in us ... be glory ... forever."
(Ephesians 3:20–22)

In June 1989, I was preparing to visit the UK. Mama had plans to visit the USA on a visitor's visa at the same time. My sister was giving her a well-deserved holiday. Mama had to delay her travel plans, as her father had just passed. She stayed and sorted out Grandpa's funeral, flying out to the USA in July 1989, where she lived until her passing in November 2011.

Frankly, I doubt Mama had intentions to reside or stay long term in the USA. We were now all adults "making life" for ourselves. The offer came, and she took it. Another "pick at the cherry!" The opportunity she turned down all those years ago had come to her in a natural way. This, she may have seen as her refuge from a shaky marriage. Our God provides in ways we'll never understand!

We Jamaicans perceive life in foreign countries to be very good. To live in England or America is the height of success. But anyone who has moved to another country no doubt knows that it's not as easy as it sounds. Yes, there is better healthcare, and other basic necessities are easier to come by, but life is tough. In order to flourish, you sometimes have to hold down two or three jobs at a time. Mama was pretty near 60 by the time she went to live in the States! Can you imagine starting a new life in a new and unfamiliar country at that age?

She moved to the Bronx, New York, where other members of her family lived. There were also a vast number of residents from the Independence City community. From a social perspective, things were not so bad. It was almost like being back home. Jamaicans living in The Bronx don't really miss being in JA. Everything you get in JA was right there in the Bronx – the food, the clothes, the vibes! Plentiful and not too expensive either. I remember during my first visit, I wanted to stay there. It was just like

Independence City was taken up and placed in the Bronx.

The weather conditions, however, especially winter, and earning a living proved challenging for Mama. We would speak regularly about how she was getting on. It was rocky, but she endured. She was always reminded that her "God was her refuge and strength, a present help" (Psalm 46:1). Being on a visitor's visa meant that, legally, she was not allowed to work.

However, my sister, friends, and associates helped find her some odd days' work in the caring industry. Eventually, my sister "filed her papers," and she became a permanent resident of the USA and was allowed to work, so she decided to enter the nurses' aide programme, which she completed over a six-month period. At her age, while acclimatizing to a new environment, she still managed to achieve this certificate in record time. I am in awe.

Nurses' aides are in great demand in the US. Most of the country is very much focused on economics. Most people work full-time jobs, or even two or three, and they don't have time to care for the ailing and the aged. I think that being a nurses' aide came quite naturally to Mama.

She'd been taking care of people throughout her life. Now she was being paid to do so.

I first visited Mama in the summer of 1993. This was my first time visiting the States, a place I dreamed of seeing many, many times. Mama was still working then. She stayed with her clients for three or four days at a time, caring for them around the clock, and then returned home on her days off.

One day I went to meet her coming off her job. She looked washed out, tired, drained. It wasn't all that surprising, considering that she was already experiencing medical issues before leaving Jamaica. But she refused to let it slow her down. She was just unstoppable.

Mama really didn't need to keep going at this pace, especially not at this age. But being such an independent woman, she felt she had to as long as she could. Numerous times, when I spoke with her and realized how badly her health was failing, I would beg, "Mama, please go back home to Jamaica." There she had her home, the great sunshine, her children and grandchildren who adored her, and she adored them. She had her church family and the community she was so established in. She refused. Sometimes I think how stubborn one can be!

I was prepared to do whatever was needed to support her if she chose to go back home to JA. Mama knew this. I told her numerous times. Mama had sacrificed her whole life for us, her children. So supporting her now, for me, was not a big deal. God had provided me with a decent job and a promising career, as confirmed in Deuteronomy 8:18, "...it is He who gives the ability to produce wealth..."

Uncle Robbie became unwell shortly after her going off to the USA. Before she received her resident papers, *he* passed on. Mama was unable to attend his funeral but made all the necessary and relevant arrangements for him to have a decent homegoing. This was duly executed by her children who were in Jamaica. Mama was deeply saddened by the fact that she was unable to attend her husband's funeral. This, though, was not an unusual occurrence. Quite a few within the community have had this experience. Again Mama turned to her God for solace, the peace that only He can give.

After that first trip, I visited her regularly. We had enjoyable times on her days off, going shopping, attending church with her and meeting her church family, meeting up with friends, eating out, going to places of interest and just spending time together.

In life, We need to be careful of the things we say! Proverbs 18:21 tells us "Death and life is in the power of the tongue..."

In November 1997, I invited Mama to visit the UK for my graduation. I had lived in this country for approximately eight years. Experiencing what the weather was like — the beautiful summer, harsh winters — I always say when I am inviting anyone for a visit, it's going to be during the winter months so they can see what life is like for us here. Well, who got that? Mama! I had to keep apologising to her.

Mama's health was reasonably good at this point, although she used a walking stick. We did a lot of exploring. She enjoyed experiencing sights she had only read about — Buckingham Palace, Shakespeare's town — I believe my mother was just so happy to see her brothers and sisters she hadn't seen for so many years, meeting her nieces and nephews she'd never met before. It was a wonderful family reunion for her. To top it off, seeing our dad was the bonus.

Mama's return journey to the US from the UK, 1998

Her first proper holiday was in 2001. My niece and I surprised Mama with a cruise that sailed from Miami, Florida, docking in Dominica — the naturally beautiful unspoilt island of the Caribbean, the Bahamas — the palm-fringed tropical island surrounded by turquoise waters, and St Thomas and St John's (US Virgin Islands). Mama had some suspicion that something was going on when my niece took her to Florida, but she didn't know what. However, she was definitely not prepared to see me, my daughter, and my granddaughter at the hotel. I do not know how the poor woman didn't have a heart attack when we arrived.

We spent two fabulous weeks together, enjoying the great new experiences. While at sea, we would go to the spa area to enjoy the jacuzzi, the sauna, steam room and the pool. Mama had some church sisters in JA who used to tell her about them going to the spa for a treat after work. Poor Mama figured that was out of her league. Now she was lapping it up. Her time had come for these pleasures. We made the most of all the facilities the cruise ship had to offer. The food, the shows, the daily activities, or just sitting around on the deck.

We went ashore when the ship made port, even though Mama's mobility was poor and she often had to use a wheelchair. In Dominica, there were some b-e-a-u-t-i-f-u-l gardens that she was dying to see. However, due to poor wheelchair facilities, she was unable to experience something she loved. That was when I made a pledge to myself: I am going to live life to the fullest, by God's grace, not put off what can be done now.

The cruise experience was a "wow" for Mama. She had never imagined having such an experience. Our heavenly Father gives us more than we ask for or think of. He gives in abundance.

Mama visited the UK twice after that, during the summers of 2005 for a summer vacation and 2007 for my daughters' weddings. She visited Jamaica for her mother's funeral in 1997 and for the funeral of one of my sisters in 2005.

In March 2005, we had news from home that Mama's oldest daughter, who was raised by our aunt, was deteriorating. Her prognosis was poor. Within a couple days of me arriving, she passed. By this time, Mama's health was not good. She was now dependent on a wheelchair. She insisted on coming home to see to her daughter's homegoing. We made it possible for her to make the journey. Again, this was very challenging, especially the terrain of my sister's home in Retreat, St Ann. Getting her from the house to the roadside and vice versa was a mammoth task, but we did it. There were always strong men around to assist with moving and handling. God provided!

It is never pleasant to bury anyone, especially burying your child, no matter how old they are. They are still your children. Though this daughter didn't grow up with us, there were close relationships both as mother, daughter and sister to us. So Mama was grateful to God that He allowed her the ability to put her daughter to rest. Thank you, Lord.

In the summer of 2005, my daughter decided to give her grandma a holiday. As said earlier, she was completely dependent on a wheelchair. That visit was challenging but enjoyable. Two of her grandchildren visited from Jamaica. It was such a blessing having them at home together. Along with my son, they kept Mama and themselves entertained while I was at work. They treated her with such care and compassion. It's funny. It was very challenging getting her upstairs to bed, but they found a way to make the activity fun. For one of them, that was the first and only time she had met him. He was born in Russia to my brother, who had gone there to study. On his return to Jamaica, Mama was in the USA, so she never met him. He sadly passed on as a result of a tragic road traffic accident in 2009.

During her visit in 2007 for my daughter's wedding, the hand of God was revealed in such a mighty way. When my daughter said she wanted Mama to be at her wedding, I thought, "No way." Considering Mama's physical condition, I couldn't see this happening. But when you trust God, "He is able to do exceeding abundantly above all we ask or think" (Ephesians 3:20). It was arranged for my niece to travel with her; she spent five days. Man, it was great! The joy my daughter experienced having her grandmother at her wedding and receiving her blessing was *priceless!*

I continued visiting Mama regularly in the USA, and we spoke on the phone often. We chatted about many things — mainly her health, which was of great concern to me, her friendship groups, her church life, and her favourite TV programmes ("Judge Judy" and "Dr Phil"). She enjoyed these as they helped her pass the time, since she was not able to go out unless taken by someone.

Mama was visited regularly by members of her church family. She spoke regularly of her pastor visiting and praying with her. She valued that. Mama was often overwhelmed at how blessed she was, as there were people who would bring her gifts of foodstuff and other goodies. Some she would say she couldn't even remember doing anything for them. You see, that's how our blessings go. It comes back to us "pressed down, shaken together and running over..." (Luke 6:38).

Mama and her youngest brother were close, very close. Even from back in JA. I guess as he was the only brother left out there, all the others were living abroad, either in England or America. I can remember over hearing their conversations on the phone. No "stone was left unturned!" The relationship they shared was so strong, to the point that he acted as a father figure to us when we were younger, to the resentment of my sisters. This close relationship continued up to the very end, till her passing. He and his family always made it a priority to check that her needs were being met. Our other uncle, who lived with us briefly in Maverley, also made regular checks through phone calls and visits, ensuring she was cared for as she deserved. Other family members kept in regular contact, mainly by phone, as they lived further away in other states.

This was the woman who was like a mother hen over her siblings.

Family members and friends would regularly visit at any time. Whether from abroad or those who lived locally, Mama was always happy to see them and make a fuss of the little ones. Even then, her caring attitude and hospitality would surface by telling them to help themselves to what they would like from the cupboard and checking that they were ok.

By now, Mama's health had declined to the point of needing round-the-clock care — just like she had provided to many clients. On one occasion, she fell and lay on the floor for nearly 10 hours. Her carer didn't show up for their overnight shift. I was furious, but God watched over her and kept her safe. Psalm 91:11 tells us, "For He will command His angels concerning you to guard you in all your ways." Thank You, LORD, for that promise which can be testified to!

I can't imagine what was going through Mama's mind while lying there. Apart from being scared, possibly she was singing her special songs. "What a friend we have in Jesus' and "When peace like a river attendeth my way" would be what kept her, knowing that soon someone would come to her aid. It was then decided she needed a live-in carer. This was organised and put in place.

A few years later, after an episode of hospitalisation, it was suggested that she consider moving to a nursing home. She vehemently refused. I guess being in her apartment gave her that sense of control. Even though Mama was totally dependent physically, she still had some control over her activities of living. Her dietary choices were of great importance. She was still able to direct, be it her carers or anyone who visited, with her shopping list. So, it took nearly six months for her to accept this idea.

Mama's physical capacity, her voice, the use of her limbs may have deteriorated; however, her mental faculties were spot on. We continued to speak regularly on the phone, although I did most of the talking. She would attempt to speak, no matter how difficult it was for her. Her carer would put the phone by her, and we would converse.

During one such conversation, she was able to verbalise through her career that "me mek up me mine."

"What did you make up your mind about?" I asked her.

"To go into a nursing home."

Shock is not a strong enough word to express what I felt.

"Give it a couple of weeks," I said, "then we'll revisit this conversation."

Mama really had made up her mind. A couple of weeks later, she had her nurse call me to discuss her decision. Since she was determined to move, I travelled to the States to check out the facility myself. To my dismay, before I arrived (in June 2011), Mama had already been moved. I was not happy, but things could not be undone.

As always, Mama was overjoyed to see me. For those two weeks, I spent every waking moment with her at the nursing home. We went for long walks on the grounds of the nursing home, with me pushing her in her wheelchair. She loved being out in the open, enjoying the fresh air and the garden.

I talked with the management regarding her care and set up what legal paperwork I could to ensure that she received the best care possible. I did request, to family members, that her pastor be informed of her current residence so that he and or the church family could maintain their visits in this crucial time of her life.

OVERCOMING

It broke my heart to leave her when it was time to go home. Little did I know that would be the last time I would see this beautiful, strong, courageous woman alive.

On returning to the UK, I rang her every day, an experience that proved extremely frustrating because often the phone would ring for long periods without anyone picking it up.

When Mama lived in her apartment, there would always be someone to put the phone to her ear, and I could speak with her. But in this nursing home, her phone was only answered if someone happened to be passing by her room while it was ringing and chose to answer it.

During her residence at the nursing home, Mama was visited regularly by family members. They, in turn, would keep me updated on her condition. They would spend time assisting her with her meals and ensuring her skin was moisturized. Mama was very particular about that.

Towards the end of October 2011, one of our cousins visited Mama. She called me to say that she did not like how Mama looked. Her breathing was erratic. I got her to get the nurse immediately and then insisted that they get a doctor to see her as a matter of urgency. On examination, the doctor had Mama moved to the nearest Emergency Room and later admitted into hospital. I was in constant phone contact with the doctor about all aspects of her care. Decisions needed to be made.

On 1 November 2011, while making last-minute preparations to go on a short holiday abroad, the doctor called to tell me that Mama was on her way out. All I asked was that they made sure she was comfortable and to get a religious person to pray with and over her.

My heart was heavy. Mama had eight children alive, many brothers and sisters, friends, nieces, and nephews, yet she died alone, albeit peacefully, in a hospital in New York. My cousin tried but didn't get to her in time. It makes me sad to know that no one was with her when she passed.

Although the last six months of Mama's life were deplorable, due to the poor standard of care, she never complained. She never made a fuss or made a scene. Though she was someone who liked things done in a particular way, she accepted with grace and gratitude everything that was done for her. Mama was experiencing that peace that only a child of God has. She had learned to be content, whatever the circumstances. She'd learned the secret of contentment in any and every situation (Philippians 4:12). She had found her peace, and nothing else mattered.

Mama has overcome. She has overcome her struggles. She no longer needs to face irate landlords, neighbours who made her life miserable, struggling to make ends meet, failing health. Nothing!

In John 14, Jesus tells us there are many rooms in his Father's house "... He has gone to prepare a place for us." Mama's apartment was ready, so He came and took her to be with Him. She is now resting safely in His arms. Praise God!

The nurses all loved her and spoke kindly of her. Just a shame they did not take the time to care for her as she deserved.

Mama's favourite song

What a friend we have in Jesus – Joseph M. Scriven

1. What a Friend we have in Jesus,
   All our sins and griefs to bear!
   What a privilege to carry
   Everything to God in prayer!
   O what peace we often forfeit,
   O what needless pain we bear,
   All because we do not carry
   Everything to God in prayer!

2. Have we trials and temptations?
   Is there trouble anywhere?
   We should never be discouraged,
   Take it to the Lord in prayer.
   Can we find a friend so faithful
   Who will all our sorrows share?
   Jesus knows our every weakness,
   Take it to the Lord in prayer.

3. Are we weak and heavy-laden,
   Cumbered with a load of care?

OVERCOMING

Precious Saviour, still our refuge—
Take it to the Lord in prayer;
Do thy friends despise, forsake thee?
Take it to the Lord in prayer;
In His arms He'll take and shield thee,
Thou wilt find a solace there.

Memories of Mama and her travels

Memories of Mama and her travels

Epilogue

Hebrew 9:27 tells us, "… It is appointed unto man, once to die." So, as a child of God, I do not fear death. The fear is not to live at all. Life is a journey, so we travel it well. Mama lived a full and courageous life. Indeed, she travelled it well. She overcame her struggles. As noted by another of Harry T. Moore's (1951) quotes: "Courage, my friend, do not stumble. Though your path is dark at night, there is a star to guide the humble. Trust in God and do right." (Believed to be from a hymn by Norman McLeod.)

My mother's story is an encouragement to me. Her legacy to all who knew her, her love for God, holding on regardless, overcoming struggles, through trusting and putting her faith in God.

Mama, you have run the race. You fought the good fight and finished the race. You kept the faith, and now there is a crown of righteousness waiting for you. And I am going to be your number one cheerleader when you receive that crown. I know there will be a host of others, but I will be right up front, making the most noise, the loudest and biggest cheer!

As I give you, my readers, this gift, I pray you will take courage in whatever you are undergoing right now, knowing you can come through this, by God's grace.

Another of Mama's favourite verses of scripture was Philippians 4:6–8. "In nothing be anxious, but in every situation, through prayer and petition, with thanksgiving, present your request to God. And the peace of God, which transcends all understanding, will guard your hearts and minds in Christ Jesus. Finally, brothers and sisters, whatever is true, whatever is pure, whatever is lovely, whatever is admirable — if anything is praiseworthy — think about such things … and the God of peace will be with you."

I hope you enjoy reading this passage and are able to apply it and see the goodness of God.

Myles Munroe (RIP 9/11/2014), one of my favourite pastors and orators, said in one of his sermons: "The richest place on earth is the grave. Why? Untold stories, unwritten books, songs, poems … are all buried there."

What a loss to society! Do not be afraid to write the stories of your life.

Let us not add to the grave's wealth!

Ruth Agatha Lewis

Glossary

Ayia, a prison yu a go mi chile, a prison yu a go: You're going to prison for this act, for definite.

Bad mine: *Jealous/grudgeful/envious*

Bush cabbage: *The cabbage suckers that were replanted*

Dem ya too lickle: *These are too small*

Duppy: *Ghost*

Fefe: *A whistle/toy which makes a distinctive sound.*

Fudge: *Ice cream on a stick.*

Filed papers: *Apply for citizenship.*

Gimme, gimme, gimme: *Give me! Or always wanting something.*

Go si dong, lef big: *Go away, leave the adult argument.*

Handcart: *Small cart pushed or drawn by hand.*

Higgler: *Person who travels around selling small items; a pedlar.*

Icicle: *Frozen fruit juice on a stick.*

Lawd, a wha mi a go do? *My God! What am I going to do?*

Me mek up me mine: *I have made up my mind.*

Mi chile: *My child.*

Navel orange: *A specific type of orange that has what looks like a navel at the top of it.*

Pimento: *Spice*

Spread: *Feast/lay (a table) for a meal.*

Stone throw: *Short distance.*

Tank: *A large concrete storage vessel. Holds rainwater for domestic use.*

Tenement: *A set of rooms forming a separate residence within a house or area.*

The macy: *The mercy.*

Took set on us: *Giving us grief.*

Uno: *Referring to a group of people.*

Yu: *You – Referring to a single person.*

Last Word

Thank you for reading this book and I hope that you enjoyed it. Don't forget to leave a review!
Head over to Amazon to
leave a review for me. Thank you so much.

Follow Lesmarie on:

Facebook: https://www.facebook.com/ lesmarie.shalan

Instagram: https://www.instagram.com/ lesmarieshalan/

About the author

Lesmarie Combrie was born in September 1956 on the beautiful tropical island of Jamaica. Her majestic confidence did not come naturally, but out of struggle, hardship, pain and, most importantly, her strong belief and faith.

A woman of prayer, with steadfast, unshakeable faith and trust in her God, she was able to see beyond her current circumstance and create a life of prosperity for herself and her two children.

Lesmarie is known for her generosity to all. She tirelessly cares for her extended family emotionally, spiritually, and financially.

This, her first book, is not just a story but also a Jamaican reality.

Made in the USA
Columbia, SC
01 March 2022

56644142R00065